✡ Not a Victim!

Thomas Weinshaus

Tom, deep in reflection, at the Shoes on the Danube memorial in Budapest 2009
  (photo by Deborah Barry)

Not a Victim!

Tales of Survival in Nazi Budapest

By Thomas Weisshaus

Edited by
Deborah Barry

Published by Jetty House
An imprint of Peter E. Randall Publisher
Portsmouth, NH

© 2010 Thomas Weisshaus
All rights reserved.

Published by Jetty House
An imprint of Peter E. Randall Publisher
Box 4726, Portsmouth, NH 03802-4726
www.perpublisher.com

(ISBN 13) 978-0-9817898-9-7
(ISBN 10) 0-981-7898-9-7

Library of Congress Control Number: 2010935709

Additional copies of this book are available at:
www.notavictim.net

Cover photo by Deborah Barry

Book cover, page design, and composition by Ed Stevens Design
www.edstevensdesign.com

In Loving Memory of

My parents, Sándor and Erzsébet Weisshaus,
both victims of Hungarian Nazi inhumanity
and
My wife, Patricia Jeffers Weisshaus

Erzsébet and Sándor Weisshaus in 1941

Patricia Jeffers Weisshaus in 1998

Dedicated to

My children, Alex and Melissa,
both serving humanity in their own ways

My aunt, Maria "Mariska" Furst Hajos,
who performed the incredible feat of entering an armed
Nazi camp to save me and her husband from certain deportation

Raoul Wallenberg, heroic fighter and diplomat
who came to Budapest in 1944 and gave me,
among thousands of others, a chance to live

Contents

Foreword by Deborah Barry xi
Preface xv
Acknowledgments xxi
Introduction by Thomas White xxiii
A Note on Transcriptions xxvii
Map xxix
The First Loss 1
News from Poland—1943 3
War Comes to Budapest 5
Summer 1944 8
War in Earnest 9
Fascist Takeover 12
Miracle on the Island 15
A Selection 18
Raoul Wallenberg's Safe House 20
Photo section 21–46
Bread of Life 47
The Price of Survival 51
Fed by the Russians 54
After 56
Afterthought 59
Chronology 61
About the Author 66

Foreword

It was while participating in the Cohen Center for Holocaust and Genocide Studies' 2008 Summer Institute for Educators at Keene State College, in New Hampshire, that I first met Tom Weisshaus. After a tremendously full and rich day of seminars and discussions with survivors, resistance fighters, children of perpetrators of the Holocaust, and Holocaust scholars, a colleague and I happened to be the first, except for an elderly man already seated at a table, to arrive at dinner. We thought he might be the speaker for the evening so we asked if we could join him. He warmly welcomed us and introduced himself as Tom Weisshaus.

Tom's presentation that evening was the first of what would become numerous opportunities for me to hear his remarkable stories of survival in Nazi-occupied Budapest during 1944-1945.

Deborah Barry in Budapest 2009

I was immediately struck by his matter-of-factness about incident after incident of close calls and losing his family, along with his strength in telling of such tragic and frightening events. I was delighted that he agreed to join our group after dinner for a session of sharing examples of what had impacted us each in classroom encounters with the Holocaust. Tom, seated next to me, freely contributed to the discussion. I found myself so moved and somehow connected to him that I reached over to hold his hand at one point—and we have been friends since.

I discovered at that initial meeting that Tom and I live only a few miles apart, so we easily got together for coffee or lunch, and as I grew to know more about this special man, I asked him if he had ever considered writing his story. At that time, Tom had already been speaking in schools and to other groups about his experiences. As a high school teacher, I had for many years been involved with teaching about the Holocaust and through that summer institute had become a Fellow at the Cohen Center. Feeling that each survivor's story is unique and critically important for us to have to refer to when the survivors are no longer with us, I encouraged Tom to consider telling about his life in print and offered to assist him in doing this.

Tom had serious doubts at the start, and at many times during the process, that his story was of any value and wondered who would possibly read a book about his life. He was encouraged throughout the process of creating this memoir not only by me, but also by teachers, students, and many others he came in contact with, that his is, indeed, a compelling and valuable story. It was difficult for Tom to spend the amount of time it would take to write down all the details he wanted to include, so I suggested that I audio-record him talking with me and during his presentations.

This became a marvelous gift to me as we sat for many hours over the course of many months talking about his experiences, his family, and his philosophies of life. His extraordinary gift also included an insightful and moving trip in September 2009 to Budapest, where Tom took me to visit many of the places that played a role in his story: his childhood home, his school, the island from which his aunt helped him escape, the safe house, the last place in which his mother and other family members lived under false papers, and the particularly poignant visit to the "Shoes on the Danube" memorial, where he sadly reflected, "This may be where my family perished." I also had the great good fortune to meet Tom's brother only six months before he passed away.

It's not all contained here in this memoir because Tom is a humble, private man. Assembling his memoir has been a journey I doubt he ever expected to take. It has been, and still is, a journey of self-discovery and self-reflection. He has learned much about himself, and very often when he and I get together he has some new thought to run by me. I am honored to have been a part of this project. Tom is a gift not just to me, but to the entire world as well.

The title Tom chose for his memoir—*Not a Victim!*—is perfect. It tells the story of Tom's experiences as a young man in Budapest and thereafter. He has lived a full and successful life in spite of, and perhaps because of, Hitler and the Nazis. His determination not to allow Hitler and the Nazis a posthumous victory has strongly motivated him for the past sixty years.

I have heard many of the students he's spoken to refer to Tom as a hero, but he's not comfortable with that term. You decide.

Deborah Barry
May 2010

Tom with grandson, Ethan - September 2010

(photo by Deborah Barry)

Preface

When, in 2003, I first began telling schoolchildren some stories of my survival during the Holocaust, members of my family who came to watch me advised me to deal as much as possible with the exciting escapes; they said the children enjoyed them and hung on every word. I followed their advice and enjoyed my success, restraining myself from dwelling on more serious topics, such as the incredible evil that could lurk in human beings and the incredibly cruel acts that this evil could lead them to perform. I stayed away from the larger, historical subjects that I was sometimes tempted to bring up.

But one day, during the question-and-answer period at the end of one of my presentations, a student opened up a subject that changed my point of view forever. He asked, "Did the Jews always have to suffer persecution? Was there ever a happy period in Jewish history?" The questions surprised me, but I quickly realized that I had been asking similar ones of myself. I had been wondering why the Jews had the image of victims, it seemed, eternally. I watched other survivors retelling the details of massacres in Poland, the horror of Auschwitz and other camps, sometimes unable to control their feelings of victimhood, breaking down and crying. I didn't like these experiences, saying to myself, "Why give Hitler such posthumous victories?" I yearned to find evidence that the Jews were not always victims, that their history showed they could, and did, stand up for themselves.

I looked in libraries for evidence of my conviction about the subject and found some fascinating material. It seems that Hitler had his dinner-table conversations recorded. At one of these dinners, a clergyman asked him why he hated the Jews so much. According to the record, Hitler responded without delay, "The Jews must be punished, for they invented *conscience!*"

Hitler's response seemed to me exactly what I had been looking for. It did not sound like Hitler was speaking of victims. He was resentful about the Jewish "invention" of conscience, and he seemed to consider the Jews a threat to his own beliefs. This was much better than describing the Jews as victims, from my point of view.

I followed this up by studying Jewish history in more detail and I soon found more evidence to give me hope. I found that from the earliest times, the times of the Ten Commandments, the Jews were a people with a particular interest in knowing right from wrong: that is, in being aware of what conscience is.

I discovered that the Ten Commandments was only the beginning. It was followed by the thoughts and words of prophets, preachers, and thinkers, among them a Jewish boy named Jesus who preached brotherly love, demanding much more than the laws of the Commandments. The universal love for other humans preached by Jesus envisioned a very different world from that of its time, the time of the Roman Empire and its Coliseum's entertainments. Were these demands on human behavior the work of "victims"?

Indeed, throughout ancient times, empires came and went, with the Jews often part of their story, always surviving, in one form or another. Empires and tyrants, Assyria, Babylon, Rome, Egypt, they came and went but the Jews went on, always holding on and being supported by their belief in God, the One God, a belief not weakened by their sufferings.

 And this is where my own story suddenly acquired a new perspective, beyond the excitement of the escape stories the children enjoyed so much. The eternal sufferings of the Jewish people, sufferings that seemed to be a school to steel them for survival against all enemies, appeared to be a mirror for me to see my own experiences in surviving the Nazi persecution I met in 1944, in Budapest. I, too, could have been a victim, but I, too, learned to survive.

Learning to survive meant more than escaping from the immediate threat of extinction at the hand of German or Hungarian fascists. It meant, after the war, leaving that world forever and starting as a seventeen-year-old in the new world. It meant making up for time lost in the night school classes of New York, in the college classes of the University of Illinois and Northwestern University, and in graduate school at Yale University so that ten years after arriving in the United States, I could start working as an English teacher, teaching native-born students their own language and literature—me, Hungarian-born but a teacher of the English language.

Thomas Weisshaus
May 2010

Entrance to the Jewish Gimnazium (academy) of Budapest into which Tom walked for the first time in 1939   *(photo by Deborah Barry)*

Acknowledgments

Deborah Barry, without her friendly enthusiasm in the preparation of this book, it could not have been written.

Thomas White, of the Cohen Center for Holocaust and Genocide Studies at Keene State College in New Hampshire, for his friendship and his years of assistance, helping me tell my story in the schools of the Granite State.

Introduction

Thomas White, Cohen Center for Holocaust and Genocide Studies

At heart, Tom Weisshaus is a storyteller, a youthful spirit guiding his life. There is a hint of something more, however. There is the intensity of his responding to injustice, an impulse to reject simplistic answers to complicated questions, a fear when hearing echoes from a past in the voices of those around him today. Voices of ignorance, violence, bigotry, and political naïveté touch him to the core. What lies behind that distant yet encroaching shadow?

Tom Weisshaus was born in Budapest on December 7, 1928, to Sándor Weisshaus and Erzsébet Furst. As a young boy, the shadow of the Nazi "Final Solution" first touched him when in 1942 his father was taken and disappeared into a Hungarian forced-labor brigade, where he died sometime in early 1943. His brother, Endre, was sent to the forced-labor brigades as well and when German troops occupied Hungary in March 1944, Tom became swept up in the Nazi destruction of the Hungarian Jewish population. On May 15, 1944, the Hungarian police, in coordination with the Nazi SS, began the mass deportation of around 440,000 Jews from the Hungarian provinces. From May 15 to July 9, 1944, more than 140 trains carried 437,000 Jews from Hungary to Auschwitz. The vast majority were gassed.

Nearly fifty percent of Hungary's Jews were murdered. Some two-hundred thousand Jews, including Tom and his family, remained in Budapest facing deportation.

After the war, Tom made his way to the United States, where, like many other survivors, he attempted to begin life anew and push his experiences into the dimly lit recesses of memory. After all, he was young, ambitious, and full of life when he arrived in New York City. He refused to see himself as a victim and found a new path. He fell in love, earned an education, found his profession as a teacher, and raised a family. He had succeeded.

Upon retirement, his distant past, in another time, in another place, with other people, began to revisit him. Although he had retired to New Hampshire to be closer to his family, it was here that he attended a play by middle school students who wanted to remember the Holocaust by telling the stories of Jewish children caught up in the maelstrom of the Shoah. Memories pushed into the background as shadowy whispers began to grow louder and sharper.

In Thomas Buergenthal's memoir, *A Lucky Child*, Elie Wiesel pondered, "Are there rules to help a survivor decide the best time to bear witness to history?" For Tom Weisshaus, like other survivors, there were neither rules nor guidance. His work in recovering the memories of a childhood stolen away and his need to witness it came upon him years later.

The tales of survival presented here echo the voice of a teenage boy whose life in Budapest suddenly became about daily, moment-to-moment survival. There are tales of youth remembered youthfully: making reflexive, not-thought-out decisions that saved his life. There is luck: of Allied bombs falling opportunely during a roundup. There are mysteries: How did his aunt help him and his uncle escape deportation to Auschwitz? There is hope: his mother finding Raoul Wallenberg. There are tragedy and pain. In these captured memories, Tom's voice reflects the hindsight of a lifetime as well as a youthful desire to reconstruct a childhood that remains clear but just beyond reach. Why pursue them?

Tom Weisshaus does not see himself as a victim. He does not see the history of Jews as only that of victimhood. Rather, he sees his story and that of the Jewish people as one of witness. He enjoys telling his audiences that Jews are often targeted because they are perceived as having "created conscience." Through this witness, his stories take hold as an affirmation of the spirit to live and an indictment of those who choose to "other" the other.

Tom never thought of becoming a witness to the evils of Nazism, to those evils we human beings inflict on the other. His witness stresses that Jews are not victims but rather targets. He illustrates that not every defeat is final and that, in the words of Michael Berenbaum, one can find a way to deal with suffering and grapple with victimization in service to humanity. History is encountered with an eye toward Tikkun—that is, to repair the world.

As a Holocaust educator/student living in the aftermath of the Shoah, I have been privileged to help Tom share his story. Students hearing him are deeply moved, schools are grateful, and discussions continue long after we have left. Yet, I often feel that there is more lurking just below the surface. I remember a particular incident when we were scheduled to discuss the ongoing power of anti-Semitism and he came into contact with a group's words that instantly brought back the reality of what he had experienced in Hungary. He was once again the teenage boy running. He recovered and refused to become a hostage to victimization. But the experience gave me a glimpse of the shadow.

I have also seen the shadow dispersed. In November 2007, Congressman Tom Lantos and his wife, Annette, were the guest speakers at our annual Kristallnacht Remembrance. Both spoke of their rescuer, Righteous Among the Nations' Raoul Wallenberg. That night, another of Wallenberg's children, Tom Weisshaus, was able to be with them to witness what a life lived responsibly can mean.

As Michael Berenbaum points out, we are in a transitional moment. Although my sons and family have met Tom and other survivors, we will be among the last to have met living witnesses.

Soon living history will become remembered history. The forces that came together in the Shoah will still be with us. Tom Weisshaus's memoir adds one more voice to the collection of witness voices that will remain as the distant yet ever encroaching shadow. We must constantly encounter this history and live responsibly as a new generation of witnesses in a post-Shoah world.

Thomas White
Cohen Center for Holocaust and Genocide Studies
May 2010

A Note on Transcriptions

The stories that follow were spoken by me to New Hampshire and Massachusetts middle school and high school students. I made those presentations without notes or outlines; they were ad lib. I showed some maps and pictures but every one of the speeches was new and different from the ones I had given before.

A wonderful young friend of mine, Deborah Barry, at one point volunteered to tape those speeches. After she had recorded a number of them, and I decided to make a book out of my experiences, she used her knowledge of computers to transcribe them to paper. Her transcriptions follow this note.

One of the photos Tom shows of himself at age fifteen during one of his talks to students in 2010
(photo by Deborah Barry)

Using transcriptions rather than written versions of my stories was a decision not easily made. The spontaneity of the spoken word seemed to me important in preserving the style of recalling the memories of the way a sixteen-year-old boy survived in Budapest. In writing, it would be my present self, at age eighty-two, recalling in the style of my present command of English. In the transcriptions, the sixteen-year-old boy is more likely to be heard, his feelings recalled more directly—and I saw this as the purpose of the whole project.

Thomas Weisshaus
May 2010

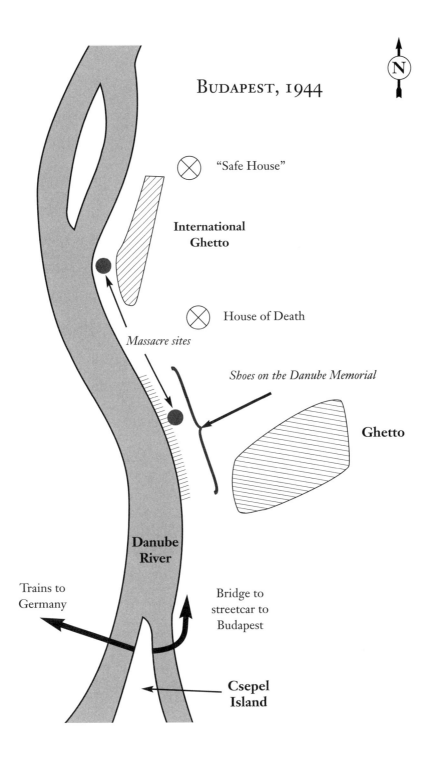

Sándor Weisshaus at age twenty-two in 1922

THE FIRST LOSS

From September 1939 to March 1944, no capital city in central Europe was as free of Nazi domination as was Budapest, the city in which I grew up. Hungarians were considered allies by Hitler (for one thing, they were Aryans) and Hungary was allowed to be an island of peace in the midst of the greatest war in history.

Even more remarkable, hundreds of thousands of Hungarian Jews lived nearly peaceful lives, while only a little more than a hundred miles to the north millions of Polish and Russian Jews were exterminated in the Nazi "Final Solution." In Hungary, anti-Jewish laws were enacted as early as 1930 by Hungarian authorities (who did not lack for Nazi sympathizers). These laws forbade Jews to attend universities beyond some seven percent of attendance, and soon there were many fewer Jewish doctors and lawyers being trained.

Jewish influence in keeping the Hungarian economy functioning was, however, never completely ended—after all, Jews, to a large measure, created the economy.

As the war began to turn against Germany, following the Nazi disaster at Stalingrad as well as their defeat in Africa, and as Soviet armies of tanks and foot soldiers approached east-central Europe, including Hungary, the Nazis had to act, because their allies were not dependable. Romania broke away and made a separate peace with the Allies. To prevent the Hungarians from doing the same (they were having secret talks with the Allies), Hitler took action. On March 19, 1944, Nazi troops invaded and occupied Budapest and the rest of Hungary.

Long before the Nazis occupied Budapest and the rest of Hungary in 1944, I lost my father— the first tragedy of my family in the Holocaust. He was taken from us because of the willingness of the Hungarian government to sacrifice Jewish men to Hitler's murderous wishes.

In November 1942, my father was required by the government of Hungary, an ally of the Third Reich in attacking the Soviet Union, to report to a train that was to take him to one of the coldest places in winter in Europe, the Ukraine, as a member of what was called the Work Service. He had to report at five o'clock in the morning.

The night before his departure I was not included in the desperate and anxious family discussion. I was fourteen and was probably working on school assignments. The next morning, when he came to say good-bye to me in the dark, I recall trying to lift myself up to hug him, but I don't think I made it. He kissed me, and said some words, but I remained half-asleep. It was a school morning.

I never really said good-bye to my father.

He never came back—I never saw him again. A soldier came to our door the following March—to tell us of his death.

It never left me—that morning—his shadow bending over me to hug me for the last time—and me, not really awake.

Not until much later did I really understand words like *never* and *gone*, and, especially, *forever*.

1943—50th anniversary of Grandmother (front center) and Grandfather Furst (not pictured), Maria Furst—age forty-seven (front left), Erzsébet Weisshaus—age forty-three (second row, second from left), Judy Szekely—age fifteen (back row, far left), Olga Furst Szekely—age forty-five (second row, right of the man), Tom—age fifteen (far right). Others pictured are extended family of cousins, an uncle, and a family friend. Also not pictured are Tom's father and brother due to participation in work service.

News from Poland— 1943

My father's departure with the Work Service on an early November morning in 1942 led to my having to leave the Gimnazium after three years of very hard work. This was necessary because my mother needed help to make up for the income lost with my father's departure. My feelings about leaving school were complicated. I lost contact with friends I had made. I vaguely regretted not continuing my education in a school I knew to be excellent but I also felt liberation from the unending homework and the fear of failure that came with that school.

Through friends, I found employment in a small workshop that manufactured plastic caps for wine bottles. I soon learned the simple tasks involved. I would have little to remember about my experience there if not for the sudden appearance of four boys, ranging in age from fourteen to eighteen, who started to work alongside me one morning in the summer of 1943.

They spoke two languages, Yiddish and Polish. Being an assimilated Hungarian Jew, I understood very little of their constant conversation. But I knew enough German to pick up some of what they told me at lunchtime on their first day. And the horrors they described were easy to remember, even to this day, many years later.

They told of the Jewish population of their town in Poland. In the early phase of the war, the Nazis used improvised methods of killing, including mass shootings of prisoners into a huge hole in the ground they were first forced to dig. But in their town, the preferred method was to force as many people as possible into the back of an army truck, lock the doors in the back, and direct the exhaust into the truck through pipes that fit prepared holes.

These atrocities, not far from Auschwitz, took place only a few miles from Hungary's borders, while we enjoyed almost peacetime in Budapest. But the following year, in 1944, our turn came.

Building in which Tom's family rented an apartment before the war
(photo by Deborah Barry)

WAR COMES TO BUDAPEST

Sunday, March 19, 1944, was a beautiful sunny day. With hundreds of other teenagers, I attended a jazz concert in downtown Budapest, at a concert hall called Vigado. It was a Hungarian jazz band playing American tunes in the usual clumsy way of Europeans trying to sound American and jazzy. One of the tunes that I especially liked, I still remember, was "The Object of My Affection." The loud, raucous crowd was young and full of high spirits. The concert ended at noon and we left the concert hall chattering loudly, to find the streets a very different place from when we left them. We were shocked to see trucks, motorcycles with sidecars, and strange uniforms everywhere. At first we had no idea that Nazi Germany had invaded and occupied Hungary that morning.

When I reached my family's apartment, I found that they had heard nothing. They listened, shocked, silent, and wondering. It took several days and several announcements that were plastered all over buildings to find out what changes we had to face as Jews. Eventually, within weeks, over two thousand apartment buildings, luckily including our own, were selected and made into "Jewish buildings."

Those Jews who did not live in one of those apartment buildings were required to move into one of them immediately. Our own apartment of four rooms had to accommodate two grandparents, my mother, one of my aunts and her husband, and me. The number of hours allowed for shopping and for any presence in the streets was announced: two hours each day. Every Jew had to wear a yellow star on his chest.

In the eastern and northeastern districts of Hungary, however, much more action of a deadly kind began to take place. Jewish people, mostly Hassidim and Orthodox in religion, began to be shipped by train in the direction of Poland to the north and, according to reports, in the months of May and June 1944, some 480,000 of them were murdered in Auschwitz.

During those months and the rest of the summer in Budapest, we lived relatively undisturbed by the Third Reich and Hungarian authorities. But activity from the air, especially in the form of American bombers, began to affect the lives of the population. Almost every day at eleven a.m., American bombers from the south approached Budapest and going into the basement became routine. Often we heard an air-raid siren at night as well, and those would happen around nine o'clock. The rest of our daily lives was relatively undisturbed.

Aside from me, the family consisted only of a few men at that point. My grandfather, who was dying of a long illness, passed away on June 6, 1944, the same day the Americans landed on Normandy Beach. We all painfully felt the sadness of his not being able to be aware of this event, a turning point in the war.

The family consisted of all women except for a fifty-five-year-old uncle and me. Often they sat around the dining table working on sewing, knitting, and needlework, which they sold in an effort to earn money for expenses. This left me to my own devices almost all the time.

During the day and the early evening, the teenagers who made up quite a number of the population of my apartment house found the lack of opportunity for activity difficult to take. We could not leave the building to find entertainment, so we had to find it inside. This took the form of dancing parties almost every night. One young couple who lived on the second floor, and who, for some reason, were able to keep an uncrowded apartment to themselves, became the center of activities for dancing parties. Because of the lack of male population, girls outnumbered the boys quite heavily. Speaking only for myself, I found the situation obviously pleasing. I found several partners to dance with, but the most important experience as a fifteen- to sixteen-year-old was the attention paid to me by a stunning twenty-one-year-old married woman who was without her husband and who attended our parties.

Courtyard showing apartment entrances where parties took place

(photo by Deborah Barry)

SUMMER 1944

*T*eenagers bored—American jazz records available—more girls than boys—no place to go (only two hours a day allowed out of the house)—parties to dance at almost every night—twenty-one-year-old married woman whose husband has been reported missing notices me and becomes my dancing partner—I've noticed her long ago, before she was married, but I'm sixteen now—the dancing gives me a chance to feel her up close, her firm body, her willing hand as she holds mine, not to mention the way she molds her hips to mine—so, soon I walk her back to her second-floor apartment (where she lives with her ever-observing mother) and spend some time in the dark staircase saying goodnight—but this doesn't satisfy either of us for long and we find other places—nothing truly intimate can happen, until one bombing raid sends us to the attic, where we must climb a ladder to the small square window—I'm to look over the neighborhood for fires (and report below if there is one)—she sneaks away from the air-raid shelter before me and is at the top of the ladder when I reach the attic—and for the first time I have help in counting 1,250 American bombers flying in from Italy.

Announcements requiring Jewish men to report for work service
(courtesy of Holocaust Memorial Center in Budapest)

WAR IN EARNEST

*B*ombings by American and Russian air forces began in earnest during the summer of 1944, after the German occupation. Soon trucks stopped at apartment houses, looking for young people to help clean up the rubble from blocked streets, or even buildings that were partly destroyed and presented a danger, having loose bricks that would crash to the street, thus endangering pedestrians.

Bombings created havoc in the city park, a huge green expanse comparable to Central Park in New York City. Having joined the cleanup crew, I walked along one of the paved roads in the park, with several others, looking for bombing victims. It was like walking into an enchanted forest. The park I had been playing in as a child was covered with smoke. Dead bodies were next to trees under which some of Budapest's residents had foolishly tried to hide. The roads were deserted except for a car here and there, again under trees. Our leader, an experienced police officer, shook his head in disbelief at so many ignorant people seeking shelter under trees and sometimes bushes.

Soon we saw a burning car that had cooled enough for approach without danger of being burned. At first, the milky windows were impossible to see through, but as the heat decreased, they began to clear. I stood, staring, trying to peer inside at the front seats. As I moved closer, mesmerized by the mystery before me, the scene inside the car slowly became visible as if in a dream, or a nightmare. Gradually, the horror became reality. For a moment I struggled to make sense of the view on the passenger seat: a dark brown-red mound of some sort of body—a large bird (perhaps a goose, the popular Hungarian fowl?) or an embryo—covered with shiny, melted fat and roasted meat beneath, inside an otherwise normal-looking car, a car I no longer saw because the view inside captured all my attention.

It rapidly became clear to us that this passenger was no fowl; it had unimaginably once been human—a living person. After a quick look, most of us backed away, but we were drawn back by the fascination of the clearer and clearer vision of something so unbelievable that we couldn't tear ourselves away from it.

Just minutes before, it was all masked by the window that blocked our vision, yet it had been there all the time, behind the glass. A human being had been caught by a firebomb and was roasting before us. As much as I hated what I saw, as much as it scared me that *that* was what had been hidden behind the cloudiness of the glass, my own eyes were drawn to the scene. Someone grabbed me and tried to pull me away, yelling, "Watch it! You'll get burned, it's still hot!" But I was somehow hypnotized by that passenger. The fellow pulling me away yelled again, "What are you mumbling?" He told the leader of our group that I was crazy as he kept tugging at me. Someone else got close to me and heard me say something, his eyes opening wide. Finally, I yielded and left the scene with them and my mumbling became clearer: "It had a face. It had a face. It was a human being in there." I couldn't stop.

It was as if the world as I had known it up to then disappeared and the only reality I could see was what I saw on the passenger seat—an unholy passenger indeed, I heard inside my head—and for long moments I lost my sense of where and who I was. Was I still the boy who had played in peacetime in the park or the boy now lost in a vision I saw through the window of the car, a new reality, a new me, a different world, a world summed up now for me by what the clearing window revealed slowly, but relentlessly, of the new world I would live in from then on?

When I returned home that afternoon I was feverish, and as my mother held me close, I asked for my father, who had been gone since 1942 and died in the Ukraine. She held me until I went to sleep, mumbling nonsense.

Marching group of work service Jewish men
(courtesy of Holocaust Memorial Center in Budapest)

Fascist Takeover

The war came closer and closer. Even though all the war news was censored by the authorities, we had no trouble following the advance of the Soviet armies and tanks toward Hungary and Germany. By August and September, Russian aircraft were beginning to appear in the skies over Budapest. This is how we reached the key month of October 1944, at which time the leadership of the Third Reich took steps to prevent Hungarian authorities from making a separate peace with the Russians and the Allies. It had become clear that there were talks going on between the Hungarian government and the Allies. On October 15, 1944, the Hungarian government was replaced by a far-right-wing, radical Hungarian group that had a history of anti-Semitism and pro-Nazi sentiments. With them in charge, Budapest's Jews were exposed to instant death, by shooting, wherever they were found.

Very early that same day, our apartment house was alerted and all males between the ages of sixteen and fifty-five were required to line up in the courtyard of the building. We were told to bring whatever food and clothing we could carry; we were going to go marching out of town. My mother almost immediately became desperate, crying out loud, "They've already taken your father and your brother." (My brother had been taken in 1943 to a work unit in the southern part of the country.) We were quickly ordered to march out of the building. I had no time to say good-bye to my friend of the summer, who was standing on the second floor, watching. We marched through the city and ran into several columns of Jewish men, like ourselves, marching in other directions. From the looks we exchanged, we knew what we were all involved in. There were also telling looks on faces that hid quickly behind the curtains of the windows of apartments as we marched through the streets. We marched out of town that day.

We spent the first night in a very cold storage cellar of a champagne factory. I searched through my bag to find something to eat and found only a can of Alaskan crab my mother had thrown in at the last minute. My uncle and I ate it, despite our dislike of crab.

The next day we continued our march until we reached a barn that had no sides, and we stayed on the second floor. During the day we were given shovels and dug ditches, a defensive move against the Russian tanks that were approaching. At night we went back to the barn, where we slept without any blankets. This went on for several days, until we moved to another location where there was no barn; we slept in the fields. One night there was a heavy rain. A moment of relief came when a local farmer called us into his cellar, which had an astonishingly large pile of red apples in the corner. He urged us to eat as many of the apples as we wanted.

It's remarkable that out of this whole period of marching, working, and being exposed to the elements, I remember most clearly that night in the farmer's cellar along with many occasions that I was so hungry I would pick up anything that looked remotely edible: carrots that were half-rotten, tomatoes that were soft and watery. We had no regular program of feeding/eating. From time to time we would have something they called soup—a dark, tasteless liquid. But I survived it.

This process of digging and marching went on for four or five weeks, ending on the muddy island of Csepel in the middle of the Danube River, south of the city of Budapest.

Aunt Mariska Furst Hajós at age seventy-five in Australia

Miracle on the Island

Csepel Island was close enough to the city to be reached by streetcars. West of the river, trains were visible, filled with men, departing toward the west. Industrially used, Csepel became "home" to some twenty thousand tired, depressed, doomed men sitting in the mud and puddles that covered its surface after days and days of rain. These men had been used for weeks around the outskirts of Budapest to dig ditches, which were used against the advancing Soviet tank army. My uncle and I, along with thousands of other men, arrived at the island of Csepel sometime in the middle of November 1944. The men sitting with me looked neither left nor right. They saw only the rain hitting the puddles. After three or so days of this, something remarkable happened.

Suddenly, an old, tired Hungarian guard appeared among the clumps of men sitting in the mud, calling out a name. As he came closer and closer, I could make out the name; it was my uncle's: Hajos. Unbelievingly, I alerted my uncle that his name was being called. We both jumped up and signaled to the soldier that we were there. He motioned for us to follow him. As we did, he led us to a small hut that was thirty or forty yards from where we had been sitting. He opened the door to the hut to let us in. Upon entering, we encountered an officer of the Hungarian army in dress uniform seated behind a large desk. He immediately looked my uncle up and down several times and asked quizzically, "Where did you find her?" Then, without letting my uncle answer, he continued more loudly, "Where did you find such a woman?"

My uncle stood as if thunderstruck, silent and shocked. He glanced at me as if to ask, "What am I supposed to say?" Then he looked back at the officer and softly stammered, "What woman?"

The officer stared at us disgustedly. "The one that was out here. The one that came to get you. Where did you find her?" My uncle could only stand there in shock. He mumbled something about his wife, my aunt Mariska, but the officer, losing his patience with us, ordered the soldier to "take these two over to the streetcars and send them home." We silently followed the guard, unable to comprehend what had just taken place. The old guard left us at a bridge and we were soon on a streetcar to freedom and life.

I knew it was my aunt Mariska who had done this. But how did a Jewish woman walk into an armed Nazi camp and manage to have them release us? How could she accomplish such a miraculous feat? Throughout the remainder of her life, I asked her many times but she never revealed any details of how she was able to get us released. I could only imagine that her connection to an influential man, a friend of our family who had connections to the government, made the rescue possible. (See the tall man in the center of the picture on page 3.) She moved to Australia with her family after the war. All she ever told me was, "I was thrown into a dark dungeon."

Those trains to the west were ominously filled with hundreds of men from the island every day. They arrived empty and left filled, toward the west—toward Austria and Nazi Germany—toward the prisoner camps. The men in the mud saw both sides and they knew. On their faces, their knowledge spoke volumes. Before we left the island, I looked back at these men, wondering what would happen to them.

They were never heard from or seen again.

One of the hiding places Tom's mother found for him—the Red Cross Villa
(*photo by Deborah Barry*)

A Selection

Soon after being reunited with our families, soldiers came and took us to a simple grass-covered clearing on the other side of the Danube and gave us the order to separate into two groups: one for those under the age of sixteen and the other for those over sixteen. All my instincts told me that although I had just passed sixteen to stand in the other line. Eventually, those of us under sixteen, along with the women and children, were marched back into the city, while the group over sixteen stayed in the clearing and were never heard of again. Within a few days of each other, I escaped from the predicament on the island and then here as well.

We were led back into the walled ghetto that had been formed in Budapest. My mother, a woman of uncommon will and intelligence, immediately decided not to stay in the ghetto, and to get me into a safe place. Eventually, she, my grandmother, my aunt

Olga, and my cousin Judy rented an apartment in a Christian building, having been provided with false Christian identity papers by someone I didn't know.

My mother hoped to hide me permanently but was never satisfied with the safety of the places she found. One place she tried was the Red Cross villa on Andrassy Street.

After ten or so uneventful days, however, she and my cousin Judy surprised me one night with their arrival at the villa. Giving me no time to pack, my mother simply stated, "We must go."

The two women almost carried me between them through dark, blacked-out streets. We hurried through streets and squares, deserted except for sentinels who sounded German. Fortunately, they seemed not to notice us, being too busy watching for approaching planes and for the occasional window where a faint glimmer of light seeped through. The two women tried to hide me between them as we scurried along, as close to the walls of buildings as possible. Audible signs of stress escaped from my mother, who was almost hysterical with the fear of losing her remaining son. My feet barely touched the sidewalk.

The unforgettable darkness—the ever-present German uniforms—the droning of airplane engines above—the unending streets—the heart-stopping alarm when a sentinel came closer and looked me over but didn't see me—a lengthy odyssey through a scary landscape—a trip across Hell!

Raoul Wallenberg's Safe House

Not long after my sudden departure from the Red Cross villa, my mother discovered that Raoul Wallenberg, a Swedish diplomat, was handing out Swedish passports on a street not far from the Danube River. She took me to Wallenberg's location, where he sat in the street behind a card table. There was a line of fifty people eagerly waiting to get to the table. Anxiously, we stood in line until I faced Wallenberg myself. He asked me for my name and nothing more. Working very fast, he got my passport done within minutes. Time was of the essence. He signed my passport and assigned me to a building protected by the Swedish consulate. Once we knew the address of the safe house, we went directly to it, and after reporting to the manager of the house, I learned I was to move into an apartment with a family on the sixth floor. I was shown a corner of one of the rooms that had a bunk in it that was to be my place in the apartment.

Raoul Wallenberg

My mother promised to bring me food every two or three days. I was to meet her at the front door of the building.

People kept to themselves in the safe house. I didn't have much contact with the others outside of my apartment. Aside from waiting for my mother, I spent much of my time at the windows of this sixth-floor apartment from which I could see the bombing and activities on the streets, and especially the growing red patches on the ice and snow that covered the Danube River, without an inkling of their later role in my family's fate.

An early photo of Endre, Tom's older brother, and Tom

Tom at the age of six

The three women in front—Aunt Olga, Tom's mother, Cousin Judy—along with Tom's grandmother, were victims in 1944.

Tom at the switchboard of the Leipheim Displaced Persons camp in 1946

Tom in New York City in 1947

Endre, Tom's older brother, at age twenty-six in 1948, in Hungary

Tom in New York City in 1948

Tom at his graduation from Northwestern University in 1957

Tom at Tabor Academy in 1958

Patricia with her young son, Alex, in 1961

Tom's beloved son, Alex, at age four in 1964

Tom at Tabor Academy, Marion, Massachusetts, in 1965

Tom at the University of Illinois in 1965

Tom on an excursion at the McDuffie School, Springfield, Massachusetts, in 1974

Melissa, Tom's daughter, at age fourteen, in Illinois in 1980

Alex, Tom's son, at Christmas in 1980

Patricia, Melissa, and Tom at Melissa's graduation with her master's degree from Bryn Mawr College in Pennsylvania

This form was sent to Yad Vashem by Tom to record his mother's victimization by the Nazis. The same form was submitted for Tom's father, grandmother, aunt, and cousin, who were also victims.

Tom in front of the Holocaust Memorial behind the synagogue in Budapest in 1999

Portrait painted by Felix D'LaConcha in Exeter, NH, in 2008

Tom's brother, Endre, at age eighty-six in 2009

Melissa with her fiancé, Robert MacIntyre, in London in 2009. They married in May 2010.

The following section of photos was taken by Deborah Barry (unless otherwise noted) during the trip to Budapest in September 2009.

The gimnazium (school) Tom attended in Budapest, September 2009

Overleaf: Overlooking Budapest

View from Csepel Island into Budapest where Tom and his uncle were held in November 1944

The apartment building on Teréz Körút in which Tom's family lived under false papers until being taken away by the Nazis in 1944

A street named after Raoul Wallenberg in Budapest

Not a Victim! Tales of Survival in Nazi Budapest 39

The front door to the Raoul Wallenberg safe house in Budapest where Tom was hidden toward the end of the war

Tom and Deborah Barry with Tom's brother, Endre (second from right), Tom's step-niece, Andrea (far right), and friend, Tibor

Rita Nagy, senior consultant at the Holocaust Memorial Center in Budapest talking with Tom

A memorial in the synagogue of the Holocaust Memorial Center in Budapest honoring the victims of the city

Display at the Holocaust Memorial Center in Budapest

Not a Victim! Tales of Survival in Nazi Budapest 43

Tom walking on a street which was once part of the central ghetto in Budapest

The entrance to the main synagogue in Budapest which borders what was the central ghetto

Marker denoting the location of the gate of the central ghetto in Budapest

Translation of the marker:

In the days of fascist rule
here was one of the gates
to the Budapest Ghetto.

The liberating Soviet Army
on the 18th of January 1945
broke down the walls of the ghetto.

Tom showing a photo of "Shoes on the Danube" to students during a talk in 2010 *(photo by Deborah Barry)*

Tom with faculty and students at Chester Academy, New Hampshire, after a presentation in 2010 *(photo by Matt Rittenhouse, Tri-Town Times)*

BREAD OF LIFE

December 1944. The bombing and street fighting between the Germans and the Russians were coming closer and closer to the center of the city. By the time I settled into my corner of an apartment in the safe house, the noise of machine-gunning and bomb explosions was almost constant.

The family with whom I shared this large apartment comprised two grandparents, their forty-five-year-old daughter, and her two children, eight and ten years old. They were people I did not know. I had a cot in the corner of the children's room—nothing more. I had to look out for myself. No food was provided in the safe house. I slept there, but was not included in the family's meals, which consisted mainly of pasta and bread they were able to make themselves. It was my mother who fed me. She risked her own life, sneaking fifteen to twenty blocks through the snowy streets of the city, carefully avoiding the Nazi guards and soldiers, every two or three days to bring me a pot of food, usually one of my favorite stews. Each day I warmed up this food and ate sparingly, eagerly anticipating her next arrival with a fresh pot of food. She was my only means of getting anything to eat. I desperately depended on the heroic efforts of my mother to keep me fed.

Erzsébet Weisshaus who had been delivering food to Tom at the safe house and suddenly stopped

Suddenly, however, she stopped coming and I had no food for several days. The family with whom I shared the apartment did not offer to share their meager meals with me, and I grew increasingly anxious and hungry. Where was my mother? Had something happened to her? If she didn't bring me food, how would I survive?

I complained to the grandfather that my mother had not shown up with food and told him of my fears of not having anything to eat. The old man replied, "We, too, are in trouble. Our oven is no longer working and we have no way to bake our bread." Their bread dough was prepared but there was no way to bake it.

There was a bakery not too far from the safe house, so I proposed that I take the dough there with the understanding that I would get some of the bread. This was a highly risky venture, considering that the Nazis were patrolling the streets and the Russians were bombing the city. My hunger for food, however, urged me to accept the risk, and the family agreed.

Without delay, I started on my way with the large pot, covered with cloth, hugging it as if it were life itself—which it was. The official sheet of the Swedish consulate protecting the house on the outside door briefly caught my attention as I hurried along, knowing that what I was doing was against the law, as I was not supposed to be on the streets and I had ripped off the yellow star identifying myself as a Jew from my coat. I could have been stopped at any moment. Explosions and machine-gunning from the planes soaring above greeted me. With the bread held out in front of me, I scurried along two blocks, away from the river, and reached a corner from which I immediately spied the bakery, recognizing its twenty-foot-long plate-glass window reflecting a large group of people, whom I guessed to be mostly Jews, standing in front of the building, all of them carrying a dish similar to mine.

As I took my first steps in their direction, the loud hum of a truck motor approached from behind me. It came to a stop at the corner. Soldiers in the greenish uniform of the Third Reich jumped from the truck and immediately began walking in the same direction I was headed. I hurried and soon saw a large army truck pulling up at the other end of the block and unloading the same greenish uniforms as the other. I was trapped. We were all trapped and in grave danger.

The Nazi soldiers, armed with automatic weapons, approached hurriedly from both ends of the block. Some people fell to their knees in prayer. Others beseeched their God in the sky. Still, the Nazis approached. I tried to lose myself in the midst of the crowd. A feeling of doom wrapped itself around all of us.

Hope had abandoned every person in the street when the miraculous happened. A bomb hit the six-story apartment house across from the bakery. The explosion demolished the building. Rubble tumbled into the area of the street in front of the bakery, injuring many, including some of the soldiers. Others were hurt by the shattered glass flying from the bakery window. Crying and screams filled the air. Blood spilled from cuts and wounds on people all around me. The street resembled a battlefield, but somehow I was unhurt.

The soldiers quickly retreated back to the trucks with not a look at the injured. Without hesitation, I jumped over the low wall that once supported the window and into the bakery, still holding the bread dough in front of me. Workers were rushing about but continuing to bake bread in the ovens. I slammed my pot onto the counter as I made my way toward a narrow corridor leading out of the bakery in the back. "Bake it!" I yelled as I ran through the corridor away from the street. My eyes were only on the way out. Behind me, people were rushing about and the moaning of the injured and dying was still distinctly audible. I was single-mindedly focused on getting out of the bakery.

Rushing through a narrow back door, I found myself in a courtyard, not the street I expected; I had hoped to be on the other block, thus eluding the chaos in front of the bakery. Hurriedly looking for an exit from the courtyard, I found nothing but a door with no handle on it. I rushed across to that door and scratched frantically along the edge with my fingernails trying to get hold of it and pull it open. As I worked, my fingernails broke and getting through that door seemed impossible.

Almost unexpectedly, the door suddenly released and I stared into a large, pitch dark hall. At first I thought it was empty but as my eyes grew accustomed to the darkness, I realized it was a movie house. Opening the door more widely, a shaft of light revealed someone sitting in one of the seats. Just as her fear-filled face started to turn toward the opening door, a young woman with long hair tried to slip down as low as possible in the seat in which she was hiding. Her shoulders were shaking with her weeping. I quickly closed the door tightly and made my way to her. Wondering to myself who she was and why she was sitting alone in this dark theater, I went to her.

As I sat down next to her, she covered her eyes, filled with tears. But when I gently touched her shoulder, she turned to me. My question about the cause of her weeping was answered with sobs at first, but slowly and brokenly she told me her story. She was a country girl sent to the big city by her poverty-stricken peasant parents. She had found work as the housemaid with a family but they mistreated her. Frightened and alone, she was trying to escape them and hid in the movie theater.

I, in turn, told her my story as I put my arm around her, trying to console not only her, but also myself in our despair. As we shared our stories and fears, we drew closer. In our need for closeness and affection, we whispered of not having any place to go.

Perhaps an hour had passed when I reluctantly explained that I had to see if I could get the bread back to its owners. I never saw her again.

I reentered the bakery the same way I left it. Rushing toward the front, I found myself alone in a deserted shop. Outside were the smoking ruins in the street and medical workers among the wounded. A distinctive aroma led me to the counter on which sat my baked loaf of bread with its beautifully browned, shiny crust. Without hesitation I grabbed it and stepped back through the window. Seeing nothing and no one to stop me, I headed back to my building, dodging bodies and rubble along the way.

I returned to the apartment safely. Sitting on my cot in the corner of the room, I began to eat some of my bread.

The four blurred spots are family members lost in the Holocaust

The Price of Survival

As more days went by without sign of my mother, I took advantage of a random chance to join volunteers working on the rubble in the streets. It became a chance to find out why my mother hadn't come to the safe house in days.

A truck came along in mid-afternoon. Darkness had almost completely settled in but I could see the Danube at the end of the street. The bloodstains were dark on the snow. I joined the group, feeling confident I could sneak away once we were in the city.

The truck rumbled along a narrow track through bombing, machine-gunning, and rubble-covered streets. We reached mid-city, where we were told to climb off the truck and report to the policeman in the street. He already had some twenty people carrying rubble off the street, piling it next to buildings.

I worked with the others as I looked for an escape route, an underground passage that I knew went to Therese Ring, where my mother's apartment house was located.

I sneaked away at the first opportunity, down dark steps to the underground, and anxiously walked toward the exit several blocks away. Luckily, I ran into no officials, German or Hungarian. When I exited to the broad avenue, it was snowing and dark. This was Terez Korut (Therese Ring), as broad as Park Avenue in New York City. I stuck close to the buildings, remaining as invisible as possible. The thick snow covered me. The street was blanketed with four or five inches of snow. I did not keep my head up so I could not see the gendarme about a block away, standing about seven feet tall in the middle of the street. When I first noticed him, he was already motioning toward me, "Come here."

I clutched my briefcase under my arm tightly and began thinking of what story to tell. As I approached him, I developed an idea, especially because across the street I could see a porte cochere (wide street gate) opening and closing all the time, and inside it a large group of people, like a beehive, who had been captured on the streets. I had no doubt I would be sent there if I didn't do something quickly.

By the time I reached the gendarme, my story was set: "I'm going to that building there." I pointed to the actual building five houses down the street and showed him the piece of dry bread I carried in the briefcase. "I'm taking this bread to my mother there, who is sick and has nothing to eat," I reported to him, fiercely hoping this story would save me.

The gendarme looked me up and down several times. He seemed troubled and glanced back at the gate: it was closed. Hurriedly he motioned for me to run and quietly said, "Run!" He turned away, but his hand was on his weapon.

I ran through the snow and reached my mother's building in no time. It was a commonplace Budapest apartment building of about five or six stories. Rushing into the vestibule, I discovered a man just stepping out of a staircase from the cellar. He came straight to me, wanting to know who or what I was looking for. He was the building superintendent. I gave him the Christian names my mother, grandmother, Aunt Olga, and cousin Judy were living under. Instantly, his face changed. He looked down at the ground and informed me that the night before, Christmas Day, a truck came and took them away. He didn't know who or where.

As he finished telling me this, several men appeared at the top of the stairs from the cellar (people were living in cellars for weeks by then because of the bombing and the fighting in the streets). They were looking at me in a way that made me start to back out of the building. The super called after me, "It was the guy, I think, who sold them their papers."

By the time I was out in the snowy street, I couldn't see. I simply began trudging through the snow, close to the buildings, back in the direction of the safe house. I had quite a way to go so I had to hurry to get off the streets before nightfall. I didn't have time to think about what probably happened.

But they were gone—forever.

It took me a long time to think about the word: *forever*. To think about losing anyone, forever—I tried to explain to people who asked how I "got over" such a loss. I spoke of "numbness"—of being in such need of food, of safety, of shelter—that I didn't have time to break down, to lose myself in sorrow. I spoke of how danger from the still raging war in the streets kept me from full realization of what happened. And then it became too late. I had to look to see where I placed my foot next, and next, and next.

I didn't yield to or think of grief. But grief didn't forget me. It waited and waited, and many years later I'm still thinking of the meaning of *forever*.

Bombing and street fighting show their signs in the city–Budapest 2009
(photo by Deborah Barry)

Fed by the Russians

Knowing I was completely on my own, I had to find food. At this point the Russians were in Budapest. A man from the safe house told me they were handing out food. I wasted no time seeking them out.

The building where I found the Russians was a large one with a vestibule through which I could see a Russian surrounded by people as he was handing out cigarettes. I was too hungry to care about the cigarettes. Behind him I saw people handing out food. The first of these slapped a huge amount of pasta into an aluminum canteen. The second, a plump Ukrainian woman, covered this mass of pasta with what looked like a red fruit preserve. A third woman, behind her, scooped white powdered sugar from a sack and covered the red preserves with the sugar. I sat down and without wasting a moment ate every bit that I had in the canteen. Soon after that, I left to return to my family's apartment.

The shooting and the bombing continued as I began to make my way back to the neighborhood where my family's apartment was. There was snow in the streets. There were bands of people, including Russian soldiers, going into and coming out of businesses, their arms full of goods. So the usual looting of a conquered city had begun. On my way to the apartment, I found myself behind a Russian soldier carrying a suitcase that made him lean to the left with its heavy weight. I paid no attention to him until he stopped at a building about twenty yards ahead of me, turned in, and seemingly disappeared. I could not help glancing at that spot as I passed the building, and from the corner of my eye, I spied the suitcase standing behind the door, unattended. Not being in my right mind, and seeing no one present, I reached behind the door, picked up the suitcase, and started walking very fast in the direction of the apartment. Not until later did it occur to me that this was probably the stupidest thing I did during the entire occupation because the Russian soldier would definitely have shot me if he had seen this.

The suitcase turned out to be full of genuine leather shoe soles, which became an unsuspected rich find. When I took two of the soles to the local black market, only a block from my apartment, I was immediately surrounded by dealers making me offers; one I could not refuse. It was a solid cube of dark chocolate about a foot long on each of its sides, weighing what felt like a ton. Most of this chocolate I gave to a relative with a newborn baby for whom she had no food. She eventually ended up in Washington, D.C., married to an American, and I was invited to live with her family for the rest of my life.

Tom with Patricia Jeffers at the time of their engagement in Chicago 1952

AFTER

I had made up my mind to leave Europe, to go wherever I had to go. I was not going to spend the rest of my life on a continent that took my parents from me. I spent the rest of the summer waiting to hear about my brother, of whom I'd heard nothing, and waiting to leave the continent.

My opportunity came when a friend of mine told me about a kibbutz being formed that was going to Israel. They were leaving Hungary on the way to Marseilles, the departure point at that time for Israel. Before I left with the kibbutz, my brother, Endre, returned from the neighborhood of Vienna where he had survived by hiding in a brick kiln. His body was covered with the signs of typhus on his skin and I put oil on him for two weeks to lessen the discomfort. He was soon at work and taking care of himself, and I was free to start my journey with the kibbutz through Austria and Germany.

Our way to Marseilles was not without its dangers. The leaders of the kibbutz had to have vodka and cigarettes on hand in order to bribe our way into Austria. The kibbutz's stay in Germany was extended beyond our expectations because of the British embargo on allowing refugees into Israel. The waiting period in Germany resulted in my discovering that as an orphan of the Holocaust under the age of eighteen, I could apply for an American passport.

Having received my passport, I was instructed by the United Nations to move to Prien, a town in the Bavarian Alps, in one of the choicest vacation spots in Europe, located on the shores of Chiemsee, a large Alpine lake. I was assigned to a room with a balcony overlooking the lake and it was on that balcony that for the first time I felt something resembling grief, mixed with despair.

One late afternoon in September, a soft rain started falling, covering the whole, huge surface of Chiemsee. I watched the splashes on the surface of the lake, millions of them. As I gazed at this scene, as if mesmerized, in the increasing dusk, loneliness descended on me such as I had not felt since that night in 1944 when I discovered that my mother and three others, all women, were gone. The thought of their being harmed, of their being disposed of I knew not how or where, invaded my already sharpened sense of loneliness and for the first time in those years, tears of self-pity began to form in my eyes—mirroring the drops that were falling, falling endlessly and falling forever—mourning all the dead in the universe, all my dead.

My opportunity to leave Germany came in late December 1946, when the ship *Ernie Pyle* left Bremerhaven. It arrived in New York Harbor on January 7, 1947.

That memorable day was made even more so by the puzzled faces of my fellow passengers as they watched the many yellow cars rushing by on the Westside Highway when we neared our pier. Fortunately, I was on hand to explain to them that in America, ambulances were painted yellow, and knowing what we knew about violent shootings in American cities like New York, we should understand that those yellow cars were carrying victims to hospitals. Fortunately, my fellow passengers never saw me again after we disembarked.

I spent three of the best years of my life in New York City, getting a high school diploma in night school, working full time, playing chess, seeing many movies. New York remained my ideal city long after I left it to work my way west, toward California. While in Chicago, in 1952, I met my future wife, Patricia Jeffers, and married her on June 25, 1952.

Patricia was convinced that I should begin my college education immediately, and her having a well-paying job made it all possible. I attended the University of Illinois branch in Chicago for two years, and received a scholarship that helped me transfer to Northwestern University in Evanston. After receiving my BA in 1957, I accepted a full-tuition fellowship for a master's degree in teaching English at Yale University in New Haven, Connecticut.

My teaching career began in 1958 at Tabor Academy in Marion, Massachusetts, and continued at the University of Illinois in 1965. Following this, I taught in various locations until 1991, as probably one of the few Hungarian - born English teachers during this period.

After a lifetime of not speaking publicly about my Budapest experiences, an unexpected opening was provided in a small New Hampshire town, Nottingham, where the middle school advertised the production of a play at the school called *Under a Yellow Star*. Under the leadership of a drama teacher and editor, Anne Sheehan, the middle school students acted the parts of children who lived during the Holocaust and from whose journals they were given passages to read or perform in the play. Ms. Sheehan invited me to answer questions at the end of the first performance. This appearance on the stage turned out to be the beginning of my new career. With my wife at my side, we appeared in many seacoast schools telling my story.

I began to give talks about my Holocaust experiences to schools in the Dover, New Hampshire, area in 2003, and have since spoken at a number of high schools and colleges about the subject.

Tom at the Shoes on the Danube memorial in Budapest 2009

(photo by Deborah Barry)

Afterthought

The preceding stories have become my means of following Elie Wiesel's dictum: If you listen to a witness, you may become a witness yourself.

This activity, of telling my memories of the struggle for survival in the Budapest of 1944, has become a reason for living. After some forty years of teaching English, I have found a new subject: the reasons for being proud to be a Jew.

My rewards are the eager faces of schoolchildren as they enjoy my stories of narrow escapes and sometimes incredibly good luck. Their responses—their gratitude expressed in writing, through applause, and with hugs—have been a great motivation for me to go on as long as I can.

CHRONOLOGY

1928
Thomas Weisshaus is born on December 7.

1939
Thomas enters Budapest Jewish Gimnazium.

1942
Sándor Weisshaus, Thomas's father, is called into the Hungarian Work Service, then transported to the Ukraine. He dies of malnutrition, mistreatment, and illness in February 1943.

1943
Thomas quits school and becomes employed in a local factory to help his mother, Erzsébet, with income. Brother Endre Weisshaus enters the Work Service.

1944
On March 19, Nazi Germany occupies Hungary, as Soviet forces enter Hungarian territory from the east.

In March—October, Thomas and his family spend the summer in a "Jewish House" (a house that contains only Jews).

On October 15, Hungarian fascists take over the Hungarian government and require Thomas and his uncle Laszlo Hajos to leave for the Work Service around Budapest, digging ditches to protect against the Soviet tank army approaching the city.

Thomas and his uncle end Work Service on Csepel Island, in the Danube River, along with some twenty thousand other Jewish men, spending days and nights waiting for an unknown purpose.

On the west side of the river, trains filled with Jewish men are leaving for the west. On the east side of the river, streetcars can be seen stopping, then going north to Budapest.

Thomas and his uncle are called into an officer's hut. The officer tells a soldier to take Thomas and his uncle to the streetcar stop and send them back to Budapest.

In November, Thomas and his uncle are reunited with their family in Budapest.

In November, Erzsébet places Thomas in a Red Cross villa to protect him from the Nazis. Laszlo Hajos and Maria, his wife, enter the Budapest ghetto in the center of the city, where they live until liberation in January 1945.

Erzsébet and one of Thomas's cousins, Judith (age 16), lead Thomas out of the Red Cross villa just before a Nazi raid and take him to an apartment in which the family is hiding under false Christian papers. The family at this point consists of Erzsébet; her slightly older sister, Olga; Olga's daughter, Judith; and grandmother Regina Furst.

On November 15, Erzsébet takes Thomas to a street in District V, where Raoul Wallenberg, a Swedish diplomat, is signing Swedish passports for Jewish individuals trying to hide from the Nazis, both Hungarian and German. Wallenberg signs a passport in Thomas's name.

Erzsébet takes Thomas to the house protected by the Swedish consulate in District V, a "safe house." She leaves him there, with the understanding that she will supply him with food that she will prepare in the Christian house the family is living in. They are living there illegally and are risking their lives in doing this.

On December 26, Thomas, without food for several days, goes into the city to look for his family in the Christian house. When he gets there, the superintendent tells him that on the previous night his family had been picked up by a truck and have disappeared. He also tells Thomas they were betrayed to the Nazis by the same man who sold them the Christian identification papers.

On December 27, Thomas escapes from the safe house with the help of an old man who knows how to cross over to the Russians. The Russian soldiers are two blocks from the safe house, and Thomas reaches them safely.

On December 28, Thomas returns to his family's apartment (the one they were renting before the October 15 Nazi takeover).

1945

In June, Endre Weisshaus returns from the Vienna area, where he survived the liberation in a brick kiln.
Thomas decides to leave Hungary and joins a kibbutz that is leaving for Germany on the way to a ship in Marseilles.

1946

Thomas spends most of the year in Leipheim, a displaced persons camp, waiting for the trip to Marseilles. He is employed by the United Nations as a switchboard operator.
Thomas applies for an American passport. When he gets it, he is scheduled to leave for the United States in December from Bremerhaven, Germany.

1947

Thomas arrives in New York City on January 7.

1947–1950

Thomas goes to night high school while holding a job and gets his diploma from Washington Irving High School.

1951

Thomas arrives in Chicago on his way to California. He works as a window dresser in a State Street store to earn money for the trip.

In October, Thomas meets Patricia Jeffers at a dance and decides to stay in Chicago.

1952

On June 25, Thomas and Patricia are married in Chicago.

1953

In September, Thomas enters the Chicago campus of the University of Illinois at Navy Pier.

1955

Thomas is accepted at Northwestern University as a junior and receives a scholarship.

1957

With a full-tuition Ford Foundation Fellowship to Yale University, Thomas and Patricia move to New Haven, Connecticut.

1958

Thomas gets a master of arts degree and begins teaching English at Tabor Academy in Marion, Massachusetts.

1961

Son, Alexander Weisshaus is born in New Bedford, Massachusetts.

1965

Thomas accepts an instructorship in English at the University of Illinois, Circle campus, and the family moves to the Chicago suburb of Brookfield.

1966

Daughter Melissa Weisshaus is born in La Grange, Illinois.

1970-1991

Thomas teaches English at the university and high school levels, until his retirement in 1991.

2003

Patricia and Thomas move to Dover, New Hampshire, to be closer to their daughter, Melissa, who lives in the Boston suburbs. Thomas begins to give public speeches about survival during the Holocaust.

2007

Patricia Weisshaus dies of lung cancer on March 15.

2009

Thomas begins work, with the assistance of Deborah Barry, on his memoirs of survival.

2010

Endre Javor (Weisshaus), Thomas's brother, dies in Budapest on April 20.

September 2010: Tom's first grandchild, Ethan, born to his daughter, Melissa, and her husband, Robert.

About the Author

Thomas Weisshaus was born in Budapest and lives in Exeter, New Hampshire. From 1947, the year of his arrival in the United States, until 2003, he incredibly did not speak publicly about his Holocaust experiences. Mr. Weisshaus was motivated to begin telling his story when he became part of the Nottingham Middle School's (New Hampshire) production of *Under a Yellow Star* (compiled and directed by Anne Sheehan), and has since travelled to numerous locations in New England, telling his story of survival to both school children and adults. On all these occasions, his wife of fifty-five years, Patricia Jeffers Weisshaus, accompanied him, kept smiling, and helped him with her advice, until her death in 2007.

Following one of his presentations in Keene, New Hampshire, a member of his audience, Deborah Barry, a Fellow at the Cohen Center for Holocaust and Genocide Studies, offered to tape his speeches with the purpose of turning his stories of survival into a book. With Ms. Barry's essential collaboration, the stories found expression in printed form, and this memoir took shape.